D0535622

What Can We Do About TRASH AND RECYCLING?

Lorijo Metz

WE RECYCLE

PowerKiDS press™

New York

Dedicated to Tod Cossairt, a true Bioneer!

Published in 2010 by The Rosen Publishing Group, Inc.
29 East 21st Street, New York, NY 10010

First Edition

Editor: Amelie von Zumbusch
Book Design: Kate Laczynski
Photo Researcher: Jessica Gerweck

Photo Credits: Cover, p. 10 © www.istockphoto.com; back cover graphic © www.istockphoto.com/Jan Rysavy; p. 4 Tyrone Turner/Getty Images; p. 6 © www.istockphoto.com/Roger Milley; p. 8 American Images, Inc/Getty Images; pp. 12, 14 Shutterstock.com; p. 16 Jyrki Komulainen/Getty Images; p. 18 Chris Whitehead/Getty Images; p. 20 Steve Winter/Getty Images.

Library of Congress Cataloging-in-Publication Data

Metz, Lorijo.
  What can we do about trash and recycling? / Lorijo Metz. — 1st ed.
     p. cm. — (Protecting our planet)
  Includes index.
  ISBN 978-1-4042-8082-3 (lib. bdg.) — ISBN 978-1-4358-2483-6 (pbk.) —
ISBN 978-1-4358-2484-3 (6-pack)
  1. Recycling (Waste, etc.)—Juvenile literature. I. Title.
  TD794.5.M47 2010
  363.72'8—dc22
                                                  2008053812

Manufactured in the United States of America

CPSIA Compliance Information: Batch #WRW909101PK: For Further Information contact Rosen Publishing, New York, New York at 1-800-237-9932

CONTENTS

If we are not careful, the trash we make finds its way into wild places and can become a danger to animals.

4

Trash, Trash, and More Trash!

Trash is anything you throw away. Soda cans, peach pits, leftover pizza, boxes, and even old TVs can all be trash. As the number of people on Earth grows, so does the amount of trash we make. In 2006, Americans threw away trash that weighed as much as 31 **million** elephants!

People can **reduce** the amount of trash they make by picking products that can be reused. For example, cloth sacks and **plastic** lunch boxes make less trash than paper lunch bags do.

Also, many of the things that we throw away could be recycled. Recycling is taking something useless and turning it into something useful. For example, newspapers can be recycled into egg cartons or writing paper.

Some landfills use bulldozers, such as this one, to pack down trash. This lets people fit more trash in the landfill.

What Happens to Trash?

Most trash is dumped into **landfills** or burned. Some trash, such as paper and food, **biodegrades** over time. Sunlight helps this type of trash break down. However, trash deep down in a landfill biodegrades very slowly. Landfills and burning also put unsafe **pollutants** into our air, water, and soil.

Trash that is not burned or placed in landfills can also hurt animals. Birds, raccoons, and other hungry animals sometimes eat litter and become sick. Storms wash trash and pollutants into oceans, rivers, and lakes. Fish and other sea animals, such as turtles and dolphins, can choke on plastic bags and other trash.

DID YOU KNOW?

The Pacific Ocean is home to a huge mass of trash two times the size of Texas. This trash weighs 3.5 million tons (3.2 million t) and is mostly plastic.

To reduce waste, pick reusable china plates and cloth napkins, instead of paper plates and napkins.

Reducing and Reusing

You can save landfill space and keep our world cleaner by reducing the amount of trash you make. Buy goods that use less **packaging**. Also, look for packaging that can be recycled. Check out books, movies, or music from the library instead of buying your own.

Another idea is to reuse what you have. Decorate a used box to hold craft or desk supplies instead of buying something new. Use a broken cup to hold pens and pencils. Give old clothes to someone in need. You can also turn old clothes into something useful, such as a reusable bag. Old cookie tins and coffee tins are great for storing homemade cookies.

10

Reusing paper or picking recycled paper saves beautiful trees, such as these, from being cut down.

Waste Not, Want Not

Reducing, reusing, and recycling means less trash goes into landfills. Making goods from recycled **materials** generally takes less **energy** than making goods from new materials does, too. Finding ways to reduce, recycle, and reuse also means that we will need less new material to make new goods. This is important since our supply of materials is not endless.

Plastic is made from **fossil fuels**, such as oil. Earth is in danger of running out of these important fuels. Paper is made from wood. When you recycle or reuse paper, you save trees. Trees supply animals with homes. Trees also take in carbon dioxide, a gas that pollutes our air.

In many places, people sort their recycling. They often have different bins for plastic, glass, metal, and paper.

What Can Be Recycled?

Many kinds of trash can be recycled. For example, **aluminum** cans are recycled at factories, called reclamation plants. The cans are cut into strips, melted down, and formed into blocks. The blocks become sheets that will be used to make new cans.

Almost all glass jars and bottles are recyclable. Things that are made of recyclable plastic often have a triangle made out of arrows on them. There is a number in the middle of the triangle that tells you what type of plastic the object is. This is because there are different rules about which plastics can be recycled in different places. Most plastic milk bottles are number 2. Someday, they might be recycled into fences or doghouses!

Taking books out of a library instead of buying your own is a great idea. It saves both money and paper!

Save a Tree!

Almost all paper can be recycled. However, paper that is coated with something else, such as wax, plastic, or aluminum, is not usually recycled. Cleaning the coated paper before it is recycled costs too much.

Today, most new paper is made from trees grown for papermaking. As these trees are cut down, new ones have to be planted. It is important to recycle paper, but it also helps to reduce what you use. You can use washable cleaning rags instead of throwaway paper ones. Try reading books and newspapers online, too. Using newspaper to wrap gifts also saves paper.

16

This man is recycling an old computer. The United States makes about 3 million tons (3 million t) of electronic waste each year!

Electronics and Chemicals

Many people do not realize that TVs, cell phones, and other **electronics** should not be thrown out. Electronics have useful materials, such as copper, in them. They may also have unsafe **chemicals** in them. Schools and businesses often take old, usable computers and give them to others in need. Most communities offer special pickups for unusable electronics. These electronics are reused or recycled for parts.

Many communities also have pickups for household supplies, such as paints, cleaners, and bug sprays, which have chemicals in them. These chemicals produce pollutants that are unsafe for landfills and burning.

DID YOU KNOW?

Look for new electronics that say they are green. These electronics might not be green in color, but they were made from recycled materials or use less energy than other electronics.

18

Compost heaps make rich soil. This soil is very
good for growing flowers, fruits, and other plants.

Composting

Trash made of plant and animal matter, such as food and grass clippings, is called organic waste. Organic waste biodegrades quickly in the sun. Organic waste in landfills breaks down very slowly, though.

A method called composting helps organic waste biodegrade. Composting uses natural **bacteria**, along with air, heat, and water, to turn trash into new, healthy soil. You can make a compost heap, or pile, for your backyard, your garden, or even your kitchen. Ask your teacher or librarian for help finding books and Internet links that will teach you how to make your own compost heap.

DID YOU KNOW?

New types of landfills, called bioreactors, are being built for organic waste. In a bioreactor, organic waste biodegrades naturally.

NATURAL COSMETICS

5,000 I.U.
Vitamin E
All Purpose
Moisturizing Creme

NET WT .5 OZ 15g

FREE GIFT with PURCHASE
WE THANK YOU!

LAU
WAS
ECO

ULTRA
GENTLE O

20
LOADS

FRAGRANCE FREE!

CONCENTRATED

OXYGEN BLEACH CLEANSER

CHLORINE-FREE

Of Course it's Natural!

around
, Pets and
Environment

HYPO-ALLERGENIC

14 OZ. 400g e

BASIN TUB & TILE CLEANER

HELPS REMOVE SOAP SCUM

Of Course it's Natural!

around
Pets and
Environment

16 FL OZ (1 PT) 473 mL e

natural
-Touc

& E

Biodegradable soaps and other cleaning supplies that
are safer for our Earth are now becoming more common.

Using Biodegradable Materials

Plastic has been around for only a little over a hundred years. However, we use it in almost every part of our life. Many objects, from buttons to cars to spoons, use plastic. The good news is that there are new biodegradable plastics made from plants that are safer for our Earth. These plastics can be composted, like organic waste, rather than put in landfills.

You can also find biodegradable cleaning supplies in many stores. Biodegradable cleaners cost more to make. However, many people still want the cleaners, so companies are working to make them less costly.

DID YOU KNOW?

Some gardeners and farmers grow plants in biodegradable pots. They can place these pots into the ground. Over time, the pots break down into soil.

New Ideas in Recycling

Companies are coming up with new and better ways to recycle every day. For example, some new power plants can turn trash into energy. There is also a new recycling system called single stream, which allows people to put all their recyclables into one bin, making recycling easier. Using fewer bins means fewer trucks are needed for pickups, which saves energy.

You can help our Earth by recycling at home. Take something you would have thrown away and make something new. Turn an old snowboard into a table or an old shoe into a planter. Buy goods that are biodegradable. Making a difference begins with you!

GLOSSARY

aluminum (uh-LOO-muh-num) A type of metal.

bacteria (bak-TIR-ee-uh) Tiny living things that cannot be seen with the eye alone. Some bacteria cause illness or rotting, but others are helpful.

biodegrades (by-oh-dih-GRAYDZ) Breaks down by natural forces.

chemicals (KEH-mih-kulz) Matter that can be mixed with other matter to cause changes.

electronics (ih-lek-TRAH-niks) Goods that run on electricity.

energy (EH-nur-jee) The power to work or to act.

fossil fuels (FO-sul FYOOLZ) Fuels, such as coal, natural gas, or gasoline, that were made from plants and animals that died millions of years ago.

landfills (LAND-filz) Places where waste is covered with earth.

materials (muh-TEER-ee-ulz) What something is made of.

million (MIL-yun) One thousand thousands.

packaging (PA-kij-ing) What something is wrapped in.

plastic (PLAS-tik) Something hard and manmade used to make many things.

pollutants (puh-LOO-tants) Man-made waste that harms Earth's air, land, or water.

reduce (rih-DOOS) To grow smaller or produce less of something.

INDEX

WEB SITES

Due to the changing nature of Internet links, PowerKids Press has developed an online list of Web sites related to the subject of this book. This site is updated regularly. Please use this link to access the list: www.powerkidslinks.com/ourpl/trash/